Great National Soccer Teams / Grandes selecciones del fútbol mundial

BRAZIL / BRASIL

José María Obregón

English translation: Megan Benson

Editorial Buenas Letras™
New York

Published in 2010 by The Rosen Publishing Group, Inc.
29 East 21st Street, New York, NY 10010

First Edition

Editor: Nicole Pristash
Book Design: Julio Gil
Photo Researcher: Jessica Gerweck

Photo Credits: Cover Rodolfo Buhrer/Getty Images; back cover Bob Thomas/Getty Images; p. 5 Shaun Botterill/Getty Images; p. 7 Antonio Scorza/AFP/Getty Images; p. 9 © Bettmann/Corbis; p. 11 Popperfoto/Getty Images; p. 13 Art Rickerby/Time & Life Pictures/Getty Images; p. 15 © Action Images/Icon SMI; p. 17 David Cannon/Getty Images; p. 19 Ari Versiani/AFP/Getty Images; p. 21 (flag) Shutterstock.com; p. 21 (left) Valery Hache/AFP/Getty Images; p. 21 (middle) Allsport UK/ Allsport/Getty Images; p. 21 (right) Bob Thomas/Getty Images.

Library of Congress Cataloging-in-Publication Data

Obregón, José María, 1963–
    Brazil = Brasil / José María Obregón. — 1st ed.
        p. cm. — (Great national soccer teams = Grandes selecciones nacionales de fútbol)
    Includes index.
    ISBN 978-1-4042-8085-4 (library binding) — ISBN 978-1-4358-2489-8 (pbk.) —
ISBN 978-1-4358-2490-4 (6-pack)
    1. Soccer—Brazil—Juvenile literature. 2. Soccer teams—Brazil—Juvenile literature. I. Title. II. Title: Brasil.
    GV944.B7O37 2010
    796.334'640981—dc22
                                        2008051397

Manufactured in China

CONTENTS

CONTENIDO

Brazil's national soccer team is the most successful soccer team in the world. Brazil has won the **World Cup** five times. Brazilian players like Garrincha, Zico, Pelé, and Ronaldinho are some of the best players in soccer history.

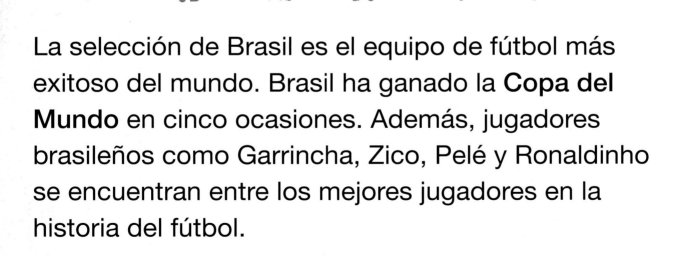

La selección de Brasil es el equipo de fútbol más exitoso del mundo. Brasil ha ganado la **Copa del Mundo** en cinco ocasiones. Además, jugadores brasileños como Garrincha, Zico, Pelé y Ronaldinho se encuentran entre los mejores jugadores en la historia del fútbol.

The Brazilian team is shown here enjoying their World Cup final win in 1994.

La selección de Brasil celebra tras ganar la final de la Copa del Mundo 1994.

Soccer is very important to Brazilians, and they watch their team with a great deal of excitement. Brazilian fans call the national team the *verde-amarela*, after the team's colors, which are green and yellow. In Brazil's main language, Portuguese, *verde* means "green" and *amarela* means "yellow."

El fútbol es muy importante en Brasil y se vive con mucha pasión. Los aficionados brasileños apoyan con todo a su selección, a la que llaman *Verde-amarela* por los colores verde y amarillo de su uniforme.

These Brazilian fans are at a game at the Maracaná Stadium, in Rio de Janeiro, Brazil.

Seguidores brasileños durante un partido en el estadio Maracaná en Río de Janeiro, Brasil.

Brazil hosted the World Cup in 1950. The Brazilian team was a strong favorite to win the **tournament**, and 200,000 fans gathered in Maracaná Stadium for the final game. However, Brazil lost the game. In Brazil, the loss of that game is considered a national **tragedy**.

Brasil organizó la Copa del Mundo de 1950. Brasil era favorito para ganar el **torneo** y 200,000 espectadores asistieron al estadio Maracaná para ver la final. Sin embargo Brasil perdió el partido. Ese día se recuerda como una **tragedia** nacional.

Brazilian player Adhemir (in light shirt, center) scored a goal during the 1950 World Cup.

El jugador brasileño Adherir (en camiseta clara, al centro) anota un gol durante la Copa del Mundo de 1950.

Eight years later, Brazil won its first World Cup in Sweden in 1958. In 1962, the verde-amarela won the World Cup Chile. Then, playing **spectacularly**, Brazil won the World Cup for the third time, in Mexico, in 1970.

Ocho años más tarde, Brasil ganó su primera Copa del Mundo, en Suecia 1958. La Verde-amarela repitió el campeonato en Chile 1962. Jugando de manera **espectacular**, Brasil ganó su tercera Copa del Mundo en México 1970.

Pelé (center) and other players are seen here cheering after Brazil's win in the 1970 World Cup.

Pelé (centro) y otros jugadores de Brasil celebran su victoria en la Copa del Mundo de 1970.

11

Brazil's success in those days was due in part to Pelé. Many people agree that he is the best player in soccer history. Pelé is the only player who has won three World Cups. He has also scored more than 1,200 goals throughout his playing days!

El éxito de Brasil en esos años se debe, en parte, a Pelé. Para muchos, Pelé es el mejor jugador de fútbol de la historia. Pelé es el único jugador que ha ganado tres Copas del Mundo. ¡Pelé anotó más de 1,200 goles en su carrera!

Pelé's (right) skill on the soccer field is the reason he is called the best player ever.

La habilidad e inteligencia de Pelé (derecha) lo convirtieron en el mejor jugador del mundo.

From 1971 to the early 1990s, Brazil did not win any important tournaments. During that time, however, players like Zico and Careca delighted world soccer fans with their spectacular style of playing.

Desde 1971, y hasta mediados de los años noventa, Brasil no pudo ganar ningún torneo importante. Aun así, en aquellos años, jugadores como Zico y Careca deleitaron a los espectadores de todo el mundo con su fútbol espectacular.

The striker, Careca, shown here, was one of the best Brazilian players of the 1980s.

El delantero brasileño Careca fue uno de los mejores jugadores brasileños en los años 1980.

The verde-amarela magic was back on the field by the mid-1990s. Brazil won the World Cup United States 1994. After winning the World Cup Korea/Japan 2002, Brazil became the first and only team to win the World Cup five times!

A mediados de los noventa, la magia de la Verde-amarela regresó al campo de juego y Brasil ganó la Copa del Mundo Estados Unidos 1994. ¡Tras ganar la Copa Japón/Corea 2002, Brasil se convirtió en el primer, y único, equipo en ganar la copa en cinco ocasiones!

Here the verde-amarela is shown after their fifth World Cup win, in Yokohama, Japan.

Los jugadores brasileños celebran la quinta victoria de la Verde-amarela
en copas del mundo, en Yokohama, Japón.

2002 FIFA WORLD CUP
KOREA JAPAN

It is said that Brazil's national team invented what in Portuguese is called *jogo bonito*, or beautiful game. Today, players like Kaká, Ronaldinho, and the young Alexander Pato continue to show why the Brazilian soccer team is the most successful soccer team in history.

Se dice que Brasil creó lo que en portugués se conoce como el *jogo bonito*, o juego hermoso. Hoy, jugadores como Kaká, Ronaldinho y el juvenil Alexander Pato continúan demostrando por qué Brasil es la selección de fútbol más exitosa de la historia.

Ronaldinho (right) fights with a Bolivian player for the ball during a game in 2008.

Ronaldinho (derecha) disputa el balón con un jugador de Bolivia durante un partido en 2008.

The World Cup will be played in Brazil again in 2014. Brazilians see this as an opportunity for the national team to win the cup for the first time in their own country. If the team wins, Brazilians can forget, once and for all, the tragic World Cup loss of 1950.

La Copa del Mundo se jugará nuevamente en Brasil en 2014. Para los brasileños ésta será una oportunidad de ganar la copa por primera vez en su propio país. Si Brasil gana, los brasileños podrán olvidarse, de una vez por todas, de la trágica derrota de la Copa del Mundo de 1950.

BRAZIL

BRASIL

Brazilian Football Confederation
Year Founded: 1914

Confederación Brasileña de Fútbol
Año de fundación: 1914

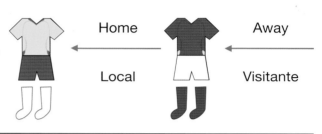

Home / Local

Away / Visitante

Player Highlights / Jugadores destacados

Most Caps* / Más convocatorias

Cafú (1990–2006)
148 caps / 148 convocatorias

Top Scorer / Mejor anotador

Pelé (1957–1971)
77 goals / 77 goles

Top Goalie / Mejor portero

Émerson Leão (1970–1986)
4 World Cup appearances /
4 Copas del Mundo

* Appearances with the national soccer team

Team Highlights / Palmarés del equipo

FIFA World Cup™ / Copa Mundial FIFA
Appearances / Participaciones: 18
Winner / Ganador: 1958, 1962, 1970,
1994, 2002
Runner-Up / Segundo: 1950, 1998
Third / Tercero: 1938, 1978

Copa América
Winner / Ganador: 1919, 1922, 1949,
1989, 1997, 1999, 2004, 2007

FIFA Confederations Cup /
Copa Confederaciones FIFA
Winner / Ganador: 1997, 2005

FIFA U-20 World Cup / Copa Mundial FIFA Sub-20
Winner / Ganador: 1983, 1985, 1993, 2003

FIFA U-17 World Cup / Copa Mundial FIFA Sub-17
Winner / Ganador: 1997, 1999, 2003

GLOSSARY / GLOSARIO

spectacularly (spek-TAK-yoo-lur-lee) In a very unusual and
   great way.

tournament (TOR-nuh-ment) A group of games to decide the
   best team.

tragedy (TRA-jeh-dee) A very sad event.

World Cup (WUR-uld KUP) A soccer tournament that takes
   place every four years with the best teams from around
   the world.

Copa del Mundo (la) Competencia de fútbol, cada 4 años, en la
   que juegan los mejores equipos del mundo.

espectacular Que llama la atención por ser vistoso.

torneo (el) Un grupo de partidos que deciden cuál es el
   mejor equipo.

tragedia (la) Un evento muy triste.

RESOURCES / RECURSOS

Books in English / Libros en inglés

Buckley, James. *Pelé*. New York: DK Children, 2007.

Hillstrom, Laurie Collier. *Pelé: Soccer Superstar*. San Diego: Lucent Books, 2007.

Books in Spanish / Libros en español

Dann, Sarah. *Fútbol en acción (Soccer in Action)*. New York: Crabtree Publishing, 2005.

Obregón, José María. *Ronaldinho*. New York: PowerKids Press/Editorial Buenas Letras, 2008.

Web Sites

Due to the changing nature of Internet links, PowerKids Press has developed an online list of Web sites related to the subject of this book. This site is updated regularly. Please use this link to access the list:
www.powerkidslinks.com/soct/brazil/

23

INDEX

ÍNDICE